heartbreak elopes into a kind of forgiving

gary lundy

Is A Rose Press

2016

Poetry

is a rose press publishes poetry, poetics, experimental
writing, cross- genre and other work. We are a cooperative
editorial board of writers in the virtual world. Submissions are
by invitation only. Check our website for updates and changes
in this policy:

Website: isarosepress.WordPress.com

lundy, gary
        heartbreak elopes into a kind of forgiving

        is a rose press
        1. Poetry. 2. LGBT poetry I. Title: heartbreak elopes
        into a kind of forgiving

ISBN 978-0-9896245-5-8

is a rose press
minneapolis-missoula

for pansy and bob

heartbreak elopes into a kind of forgiving

it is somewhere a dawn.

i cannot wait to write my hand back onto your skin. past the kind of cliché they turn into. on the radio. he sees the black and white photo. believes he can see an outline. of a nipple. although out of focus and covered by hair partially. it remains her breast. fixed on the screen. he believes. wraps his mouth around the areola. delights in this fiction. of a possible. improbable though it remains. her legs and shoulders expansive. hold on for a few movements. shiver the snow outside the window. an other noon. an other time. i ought never to have left you. he intrudes upon my body. inflicts a joyous pain. sans passion. sans desire. i ought never to have permitted him access.

there ought to be more words. to refract emotion.

a crime. to write smitten. to write illusion. as if in context love. to write distance. small breasts. to write in more than black and white film. more words like a specific pleasure. a voice take flight. land on a snow covered lilac branch. more notes to afford comfort. a mirror. a camera. long naked blond hair. a wind forces smoke back in lungs. black disappointments. to slide skin inside skin. to tongue the eyes touch. in a first time before. solitary. solitude envelops in white the cascading day. an other real noon. to write pretense. to write a self gives up. to write my life a part from here. displace death. there ought to be words. for joy only. disappear into the marginal lives. like homemade vegetable stew. unremarkable mark on the body print onto some horizon. horns gawk in the back row. key invented on some other piano. a cigarette at midnight. a stop as sudden as this.

as usual morning takes on an air of metonymy.

maybe i will let the beard grow out. down there someone licks a new recording of an old song. a change. excellence. he thinks of moving into her house. attempts at a marriage of proximity. many i wash three of four times. read maybe the marginal silence. and you would. wouldn't you. bar chord a dozen new songs. valuable. old magazines. filled with an other yet. holding a yield of undiscoverables. hold the note out past an eight count. diminish. can confusion be the modern equivalent of emotion. a motion tucked tight in a can of soup. it's something to think about at least. better than eating a frozen pot pie. while loneliness puts another worn out song on the music exchange. gruffly. better to turn it off than play outside.

she ties her shoe to the back rung of an ice cream bar.

the river widens just south of sky. when you listen carefully. a piano. solitary. he escapes memory by wrapping up containers of books. i turn toward my lover. pretend an exodus of flavor. recall ordinary fraction. like scratching your ear. i'd like you to quietly listen. go down into that dark room where secrets are forbidden. this quiet lists toward the back room. where hope covers the floor. snow dusted sidewalks. this can be all finally there is. awaking to broken glass. simmering water. tea. a piano. stuck on repeat. he bends across the table. takes your hand. she walks in the rain covering a bright fear. fourteen perhaps a lucky number. even when surrounded by sirens. a fragile truth about touch. whisper a word to name this night. elope into soil. garment dye the back into place. your lover paints with the lights out. willow touch. demur. tonight in still coldness. you rub your legs together under blankets. the mind a place of deception. my lover counts the clocks of our passage. into. an i hope to touch your body quiet.

he does not know what it means to be a man.

always the failure. always the attraction to womens clothing. once in a memory. she clowned around the older man. brush softly his illusion. about possibility. i assure my lover in letters. grace the page with a world where they belong. it is never the complexion of salt and pepper. in the night she pretends she doesn't know him. pretends he does not badger. wolves in the forest frisk a doe with consequential howls. what do you know about others wants. he needs to equate love with loss. a wonder of rainfall and snowbanks.

how to wrap your mind around his body.

in such a way as to eliminate gnawing distance. he wonders listening to an isolate winter piano. she could just move. as easy always as that. for years i refused to love anyone and thus be reduced to this town only. some days break open with a charm of improbable fictions. stand outside look deep into south. pretend a blue occasion smiles. these dreams feel raw. in some way of saying. delicate trebles envelop want. how to wrap my mind around your body until you know how beautiful i feel. pause resilient silence. a furnace clicks on in one of the houses on the darkened block. an adventure of timing. i cannot have you here and for that i grieve. he is supposed to. and that frightens you. so much remains at stake. you hear the chords progression in that distance. last night in a dream your lover said no. stark lights the horizon.

**the heart never fully recovers from heartbreak.
yet it endures.**

he thinks about your magic. that spell thrown around his body
every night before sleep. when he holds you. laps the dark night
wine. man scent. she wears braces. concludes perfection always
painful. angry i throw my arms and eyes around the shocked air.
my boyfriend. i think as the other mans tongue slaps against my
heart. a friend. i thought plaintive. predate her intrusion. on the
way to his lovers city. i latch onto the other mans voice. coward-
ice. threatening. recollection a sharp detail. detain a moments
grace. a hug. she smiles and light detaches from a front tooth.
a dove. he thinks. swallowing that last time. disgraced. inten-
tionality floats out of your book. stains the new rug. say softly.
say. dying. see crystal tears and unwrapped water. fire a cap into
the other mans eyes. wipe the counter clean. still stay the tree
limbs.

why is it that what you like becomes gauge against what she wants.

hierarchies. or for that matter. push against the wants of the stranger. lean against the books. shelved on a back wall. no word can replace this one. this time. alone in snow. sun runs on borrowed time as well. whether hidden or not. the finest truth. eliminate disagreements boyfriend. my lover studies the flying habits of self-confident boys. analog realities. she struggles over words. a hunch here is a safe bet. the subconscious terrain hideous. to stumble a pure coincidence. recollect tools. spend day house cleaning. nothing to compare to your odyssey. check cyberspace for a connecting conversation. an idea plays forward backing into a move. joy resplendent as nothing. an edition complication. from or to. but rarely at. what remains digital. tears well. my heavy eyes. for no reason. but time. her story calm. light another cigarette. feel smoke course through. in a mirror he sees her reflection. capture my imagination. available. an angle of sight. close up play thing. involve professional. all day. longing. friendship fabrication. medial. a fine eye after all. shrug off priority truth. in her blue worlds grow. a main compound. comic. flavor sweetness feathers. low.

you come into play not knowing. as image an other.

though miles apart. a piano thought. i write you into my world. to say a whisper word. tongue vowels. teeth consonants. perhaps you return a ladder. a table. stain a rug. today shower speaks comfort. shoes bring peace. a cloud covers. open. to say. repeal again. to move a move. ahead from behind. hazel pure. push lavender rose towel. against door and floor. white. nuance skin surface. a mirror frame. add color. add desire. make up surface. a sense to smell salt. sun heat. tan line. beige wonder. press knees to torso. snap another picture perfect book. a look into lens.

there is so little. to say. more than this.

smoke a cig. wipe sleep flakes. of eyes. you remain my lover. so surely. lively. to move into. next to you. he holds hands. above my head. withholds pleasure. she rocks back and forth. the open book pleasure dance. and wheat. and seeds. burnt lips cross. tea steam. tell me my name. why don't you. whisper. for a first time. health toys. heaven speaks. finally. from below. our sore soles story. succulent. my other lover. calms. walks awake into. white. instead insist. i am real. instead touch blue. say brown instead. eyes. hazel afternoon. violin. single instills. sit idle past time. last may. instead. she incorporates. in seeing him again. nostalgic displeasure. like in a childs story. the book pages flap. spring outward. a roof. music stills. a lonely time. like an awful boredom. in knowing. love does not live. forever. nor even. more than few. instants.

i wonder how you behaved when your sister died.

did you fall onto the tracks. hoping to be cut into pieces. fillet. when my sister died i stood alone. little to do or find reason for. when the small car swerved and flipped three times right behind me. i could hardly understand the impossibility. of survival. my sister would call. nearly every day. just to hear our voices. her children grow into beautiful adults. when introduced to a woman and her four year old son. he asks how long its been since her last pregnancy. words between us take on the life we can't own. where else but in a momentary. when as if time slowed down. reversed. replay her death a lifetime.

he sees the world in fragments.

looks up in time to notice the skin of the woman. the small of her back. a hint of tattoo. he smiles. returns. a disheveled blouse. white. the new haircut. a solitary hair curls into a grin on the table. it remains always the same. two men in earnest conversation. their god abandoning them with their first uttered words. they can only hear themselves speak. she doesn't see her beauty reflected. the mirror. rather all the work ahead. look across the empty street. bright light shard car window blinds. belief kills all who approach. fleeting smell of soup. sweat. and salad greens. she leaves a page blank for his comments. how to admit it. he writes himself onto that page. as if her skin inviting. climb the plate glass window. nude oblique glance. blue alaska eyes. drop anchor. bracelet atop her dangling lips. maybe you should teach her what is valuable. the two men agree. ice crushed upon a counter top. espresso machines runny nose.

you feel exposed. in the open. revealed.

it has been four years. since you felt him enter you. to the day. you realize. he comes to your bed. it is late. you pretend to sleep. after the party. after drinking too much. you will leave in the morning. your friend will drive you away. he comes to your bed. you pretend to sleep. you miss him already. i miss him already. too much. it has been four years. and he comes to your bed. after drinking too much. the party finally over. the going away party. and you listen to his clothes. as they drop to the floor. you listen very carefully. you wait patiently. you miss him terribly. i miss him terribly. already you have driven off. and he comes to your bed. he slips under the blue covers. you hear his hands as they stroke your back. as they stroke my body. you pretend to be sleeping. await his advances. i know they are coming. after drinking too much. you go to his bed. you already miss him terribly. too much. you know he pretends to sleep. you know he listens for you. to wake him. i wait for him to wake me. his fingers on your back. you instinctively move back. toward him. he wraps you in his arms. he has already lost you. he has already forgotten. the words. that would keep you there. i feel his fingers touch lightly. your chest. play with your exposed nipples. he knows you love this. having already. you leave tomorrow. you drink too much. four years ago. your friend drives you away. you leave him. he comes to your bed. before. even though you have already left. you feel his fingers as they probe. seek that entrance you love about him. i pretend to be sleeping. even though i move closer to his body. he feels your insistence. pushes steadily. opens you like the hidden nest you become. you cannot resist. you moan softly. when he takes you like this. you wish your friend had not driven you away. when he takes you like this. he wishes he could remember the words. that would keep you here. he feels vulnerable. exposed. he comes to your bed. you pretend to be sleeping. he has already left. you let your clothes fall to the floor. enter into his dream. he welcomes you. wills you inside him. listens for the words you have forgotten. for hours. even after morning light cracks open. the room. he remains inside you. moves without caution. to drive you away. you move your body. with his. even after morning light breaks open. the room. you pretend sleep. your eyes closed. when he feels himself deep inside you. the sound of one lost word. tries to surface. then dissipates. you feel him deeply inside your body. so near your heart. so near the whole of this last night. i feel exposed. lie. he moves against. and with you. you pretend you are sleeping. his arms wrapped tightly. around your body. your nipples harden. he hardens inside you. resolved. he has forgotten the words. that would keep me there. you wait. but cannot prompt him. your friend drives you away. you glance back. he stands by the door.

i dabble on the cusp of an idea.

my lips. you come to me. briefly put to the tip. you lie toward me. my tongue. one slight touch. you remember. imagine more. i take my time. my lips. my tongue. you arch your back. i pin your legs. my torso all they know. my fingers. you close your eyes close. my lips. whisper against. my tongue slow movement. you harden against our possibility. my tongue. light licking. you move away from imagination. my tongue along the shaft. you finger my head. i speak an open vowel. wrap mouth slowly around. tongue split end exaggeration. you willow. branch down toward my lips. my tongue. my secret. inside we may become more. all night. this night. my lips. my tongue. i turn you into want. into instinct. into love. this night. all night. deep swallow choke. deep penetration love. deep together.

it may feel like you are about to do something terribly important.

the first important thing of your life. it may feel like a writing. you know he is about to die. like an idea held too private. released in the daylight air. she folds her body in such a way as to mirror the frame. it can never last that long. since you chose to move. everything has changed. he no longer looks on your body. the desire once present is gone. she sits across from the man. laughs together. to want is about to leave his life forever. he walks into a new room. the mute button pushes hard. you stretch out on the couch. arms pulled taut above your head. he proceeds as if already having memorized their night. already. she dreams of a world. where she doesn't fit so well. too well. resumes a walk away. representation distance. he looks into the mirror. feels his hands on your shoulder. rude dusk like light. gray. rose. when he comes into you. the body speaks a truth about grace. he wants you. to remain in him all night. before the morning light shatters the room. they remain awake. she wants you to believe in purity. pours over bound editions of their voices. you reach back into a time. feel his warm breath on your neck. bend over to bring him back into you. again light floods the room. warrants go un-served. your heart bursts into orange. blue. your arms grasp his hips for deeper pressure. lift my legs like you want. the woman i become.

one awaits. an arrival. a movement or two prior.

one awaits. more. a more than mere. a more than words trans-
planting this. a reality. even when solitude masks. my holiday
crowds. of strangers. sipping coffee. he licks the cups edge. his
lover edging into your bed. earlier. morning stark hours caroling
elopement. he resides. stares calm. a face in face. he breathes
in moistness. the mans voice all around the walls. every bodies
business. he cares. you remain apart. by years. hours.

and quickly you recede.

you move backwards. into shadow. the walls surfaces. take flight. no more hands on my head. no more arched back. no more small drops on the end. to lick. i am left. to lick. the night air. this night. the surrounding silence. my arms heavy with empty desire. to round an oh. my moist lips. to speak a word. my tongue. to close my eyes. to imagine brown. to imagine blue. to imagine an us fabricated out of desire.

he is lost. i am lost. in amazement.

an old woman. with an older man. bent in youthful energy. bent toward each others lips. a lisp falls effortlessly from his side. she giggles. as he wraps her virginity in his disinterest. desire stays warm. inside. he is lost. as am i. as you go down on him. on my knees. i watch. alert. amazement mounts. a lisp falls from his side. while she hardly bends to reach the floor. i take it all in. as you do your lover. as i do. the couple looks still at each other. she reaches farther than her dream. where he flees into a forbidden. he hates me. he hates that i stand in amazement. that i might understand. that i do. you take him deeply. your mouth. a sudden reflex. to understand the old mans reticence. how he still resists. dreams of a rocky shore. a rock strewn love affair. i am lost. as is he. the amazement factor. our bodies. his and mine. she remains in frustrated silence. to prove her strength. she takes his face in her arms. rocks back and forth. unequivocal she understands. what she pretends is at stake. after so many years. so many lies. words now flood the room. where we stand or kneel. in a moment. one more movement. he is lost. my mouth surrounds him. she weeps in willow threads. amazement follows after us. bites at our ears. tries to sway direction. now necessary.

you find it impossible to understand.

why he finds your black and white photographs haunting. as if he cannot retrieve what is already lost. what has always been lost. in the mirror he mimes your pose. to see how close you can be. yet he always frustrates the moment with language. words spill around his naked body. my lover sleepwalks through the day. to awaken his desire for me. he drinks slowly. inexpensive red wine. that is all i remain to him. inexpensive red wine. domestic. she envelops your day in laughter. two women speak closely about art and rage. their husbands abandoned to thoughts about themselves. my lover writes on the walls of canvas acrylic dreams. where my absence floats. as if above a festive parade. or a row of black sedans. funereal. parade. the man has died suddenly. music diminishes. thwarts understanding. kneeling in front of the mirror he envisions her photograph. loves himself thus abstractly. my lover lies beside me. his hands stroke my body. covers it with bruises. encroaches memory. a piano listens from an adjacent room. pillows fall to the floor. you take him into your arms. hope to ease despair. his losses weigh heavily on your shoulders. your bare skin. i turn to look into my lovers face. count the beautiful brown eyes. equilibrium. you wave your camera in the air. accidental shutter speed. he peels a grin back to reveal a nothing as large as your body can bear.

he sits holding his head between his eyes.

as if grief accompanies a piano. he moves his face to his hands. rubs between his eyes. an echo crying. pulse beats against another barrier. where do you think he's been. perhaps you think he writes. is a writer. but how to know. he rests head. forearms crossed beneath. fatigue engulfs the room. as if evening light could not be enough. in his posture confusion springs. what can it possibly mean. he hears someone watching. someone who will claim authority. knowledge. you want him to look up. to show interest. yet he remains. unremoved. in the shadow quilted room. a time for reading.

you recoil from the image.

it is not her face or body you flee from. it's like a presence. a
likeness. last night a lover wrapped you in his arms. played. you
almost felt beautiful. today you await the attack that always
comes. it can be merely nerves. or something more dreadful.
like ice encased flowers. she talks about saving him. a friendship
built out of scraps of distrust. the day lights brightly. voices sing
in laughter. a piano dances in the background as if unimportance
counts. the writer never displays an understanding of the world.
rather lives within confines of imagination. occasional memo-
ry. you know he wants to destroy you because the indifference
balloons. wander in a breeze. green. like an advertisement. you
begin to be able to retrieve solace.

he feels a meager sense of place since he left you.

when you left late that night he crumpled the words he'd strewn around his house. to protect from loving her. threw them outside caught among the fallen poppy blossoms. no plans can ever be made to sustain. he watches the writer busying himself outside the world. begins a wish. sets the cup down. looks ahead. pain follows deliberately. the loss enormous. final. you will never see him again. having driven off he understands his world stood outside change. transformational. return to sleep. hope to find a world to be safe in.

he listens as the other man impresses.

language cracks open the air. new light. new life. he sits observing. his life lived openly. as only a reader. unkind. ineloquent. she lives beside his body. unquenched desire. sun motions others outside. smoke break. he looks at her face. her glasses and nose. her ears. how the shoulder blades lead inside her dress. he can neither resist nor accustom himself to such unclothing. outside desire blazes. his lover lives thousands of miles away. hides in his studio painting his love onto canvas. onto the impossibility. i break to permit silence as touch interrupted. the side of your breast. scar. breathe. the young lover speaks couplets into your coffee. apologizes. your eyes follow her neck. she speaks kindly. do you know what it means. he watches you and awaits action. a mere shoulder shrug. a sign. there are times when a day unfolds until it suddenly shuts down forever.

you sit at the counter. reading.

maybe jane austen. maybe george sand. it doesn't really matter. it's early sunday morning. two children play beneath the second booth. their mother addicted to them. as she has been before to a needle. he watches you reading. hears your laughter sparkle. notices you don't shave. your skirt old. my lover paints agony in the attic of loss. suffers acrylic dreams. imperfect images. he sits without asking. turns his back. you wander as you read. imagine an other coming to you. coming into you. the writer depends upon what is heard. red cup and saucer. imagine a truer laughter. like a two year old. he sits watching the beautiful young man. behind the counter. whose voice lilts and tugs. whose eyes betray sorrow. a song slaps your book closed. chases out the door.

he doesn't know what he is supposed to do.

how to act. or when. with her. as she sleeps he dreams of alien terrain. how his body might be able to. his body disappoints. before. disgrace companions this distance. once. in a memory he gave in. felt soft skin. moistened by night air. lavish is saying nothing like again. that night she smiled. took over. uncovered roots and fears. he sleeps fitful. alarm glow. proximity. diamonds. she already has forgotten how beautiful they were. where to find the thread that would unravel all of this. not even rain. not even essential. no fate involved. planets orbit. the clock hands circle. he sees in his body hers. wishes it into being. a young man smiles in uncertainty. for him. the only question remains. how not to be left alone. he believes in the happy family. impossibly masked. the writer struggles in the midst of visions too complacent to ever matter. my lover watches as i sleep. momentary hesitation. then slides next to me. into my sleep. into my body. heartbreak elopes into a kind of forgiving. like a forgetting. never before made.

tonight i am writing into you.

as if in conversation. the voices mingle. sound alike. you are broken hearted. alarmed by the flood of feelings. despair. i can only hold you. comfort. wrap you onto the page. prevent more danger. but it's already too late. suddenly i find only my voice. have lost yours. have not been careful enough. can not feel. do not notice you pulling away. how fear leads you off. chained. blindfolded. tonight our bodies feel warm together. and then it's over. timeless. terrible and awake. not even fear. that moment before memory. you watch as his image shrinks in the rearview mirror. or is erased. behind a dozen houses. but gone. remains. and a never again. to prove it. to ride it out onto the roads asphalt. a sidewalk maybe. of a woman whose look into a mirror will regard forever differently. the camera. a piano. a color. say blue. say brown. hazel. you dream your lover and you dance. in front of everyone. even strangers. and because you are in his strong arms. safety. outside she wonders. the writer folds hands. maybe thinking surrender. maybe wondering how quickly ink dries. dies. my lover follows the canvas as it leads his imagination. or maybe he drinks. the solitude of red wine. with all the windows open. with a whispered breeze. or maybe like you. my lover forgets. more truly cannot understand. how permanent departures are. i look at the black and white photo. and you look back in astonishment.

he sometimes smiles.

like an accidental joke. today the writer watches as you sit at the counter. legs crossed. top one keeping time. unconscious. piano. you are like the writer. while my lover pretends silence is his friend. turns the radio on high. there's a young man so full of what he has to say. to you. you nod. disinterest breathes over your body. his words spill all over the floor. ink rains. cool spring air. a bird or two. my lover affixes ropes to the easel. a simple precaution. for my return. she sleeps alone pretending her dreams promise pleasure. today. rain. ears. instead of entering into life. the writer looks on. a solitary crow. perched atop a telephone pole. one time he becomes another story. he waits. desires approach. the writer notices. thus misses everything. you might reveal in a self-portrait a vulnerability in hiding. my lover repeats a name back into his bed. i lie awake in disturbing dreams. a sound of metal on glass. repetition scrapes against crusted eggs. shells permeate. solitude sings the piano keys. proceed ambulatory absence. instead regard her still smile. in the camera lens. go back to that time. eliminate the following days. feel finally free. a kind of expansive. and balloons.

it is and to kiss. interrupted.

noise and playful banter. take another picture. a photo of you. winnow mirror talk. he rubs hot water over his hands. his fingers spread. long. beautiful. a color of rich soil. i wander through his imaginative garden. kiss the petals. his lips. behind each ear. he plays dead. roles me onto my back. we release a pleasure bright spring sunshine. she ruptures every straight line. disrupts romance. interrupts the preacher sons inspiration. tonight you go out on a date. the foreign polite conversation. a young man acts out contemplated poses. remains a whirlwind of indulgent energy. it may be we all love our lives too much. ply it to breaking point. i walk into your arms. sink my head on your torso. plead for you to come back. forget it all before we know it's been lost.

you look familiar.

a friends friend perhaps. an ordinary face. it could be anything.
so long as you remain ignorant. it is a loud room. voices rage
against each other. not even the piano is able to cut through
such despairing silence. you begin to cross yourself. feel the gen-
tle touch. soft cloth against your smooth legs. you understand
the unattractive nature of your beauty. you know you must love
a woman. mens constructed desire for beauty what it remains.
unimaginative. the writer struggles with his food. wonders if he
too is about to die. what would my lover say to such a thought.
my lover would flee back into denial. his studio. take your time.
enjoy the setting. find a fitting laughter. remain present. no. no.
no. you keep repeating to yourself. an eternal prayer. figurative.
furtive. in the black and white photo she weeps. just beyond the
cameras frame. he touches you lightly. afraid of disturbing the
moment. call it intuition. i am leaving. it is a return we grope
madly every night. after midnight.

she lies to the side of the room.

set apart from you. who stand alone as well. a middling this. her back toward you. the bend a transformed question mark. knees pulled toward her breasts. he wonders what to do. whether or not something is wrong. an illness. certainly difference blends with the rooms light. a difference the size of a small book. his thoughts consume. he notices her long fingers. fidgeting with the waist of her skirt. her legs bare. shoulders. could it be possible to imagine this episodic performance. hers. he doubts. aflame in continuity he boxes in fear. approaches only until his shadow lies on her right foot. a moment. like a pleasure.

he doesn't mind the world now that he's removed his glasses.

forgotten where he placed them. carefully. he doesn't mind the soft edges of things. even though they are lost in the fur of blindness. at the restaurant he admires the waitresses legs. thinks upon them with envy. fervent desire springs ineloquent. once again. without asking your permission. my lover stands in the shower. his head under hot stream. he hopes this will help ease the dark hole in his heart. she walks in colors. laughter rings circle around her skirt. i've always been jealous of you. your hands and fingers. when my lover bends me over the bed a universe unveils. a majority rule. we are all thus the same. in the alley metal fire escapes perch above trash cans. a community moment. an isolated wooden frame holds discarded cardboard. why ask. such simple rules. she lies on her bed. awake to improbabilities. in the arrival of another. my lover looks out onto the empty street. rain. one red light. darkness. hopeless cause. last a few more minutes. stand still water falls. the writer never knows what may be found among the words strewn upon the page. those sudden jewels.

my body is no longer illuminated.

as a boy you remember laughing. she dances naked among black and white photographs. photos of another posing. my lover swims against flood water. gasps for breath. two older men sit upon the canvas acrylic covered. a childs high pitched voice carries along the wind. piano notes accompany. polite conversation. contrapuntal. when the moon rises above roof tops. when a phone rings in some distance. you will pretend. to shave your body into her shape. forgive for a moment. age. outside. spring snow. heavy. a wonder. to sing a carol of longing for any other. repetitions. we buy the mask of incompleteness. waver between shadow and light. my lover leans toward me. his lips full. his tongue tipped ripe. the writer dozes off in a large cloth armchair. assured of missing little. you look my way and a heart softens in ohio. the writer rests on reputation. like a second language. a further home. lost in the photos. desire. to write a consequence. beyond childhood. my lover stands in front of me. lifts his right arm above his head. as if reaching for a promise. my eyes languish on his bare chest. muscled arm. think a minute more. before you imagine. to speak. live crushed. too late perhaps. you wander streets empty silence.

.

you watch the two young women.

who talk in earnest intimacy. there's little more to say. you cover your eyes. pretend to read. but listen. their close attachment palpable. palatable. you eat each their bodies. you sit still. in pretense. reading. my lover flushes flood water onto the saturated ground. outside the basement window. his presence illumines the day. snow. heavy spring. can dash hope. you forget you are watching. the two young women. caught in intimate conversation. you imagine their bodies. their clothing masks interest. my lover stands over the sleeping body. i cry out. the pain. dream a fantasy. i don't know where i am. nor how. what. you reach across the separating space. take one of their hands. in yours. they fail to notice. i remark with my eyes the gray sky. right now a piano lies dormant. soundless. except a whisper. of promise. these two young women. these two lovers. oblivious. caught in their comfortable bodies. you rub one of the hands. slowly. you feel their heat. their indifference. you might have been born only for this. she sits on the floor. lifts her shirt over her head. pauses. floats the shirt around her neck. head. looks into the mirror. as if at you. her eyes open. unhidden. my lover begins. lies down beside the sleeping body. he licks my back. slow currency of desire. i cannot remain still. the body shudders. breaks out in goose bumps. it may not be cold. she forgets all about your eyes. the camera. listens intently toward their conversation. my lover flatters the inert body sleeping. speaks close words onto skin. acrylic beads. sweat pools on the covers. the room darkness cloaks.

i imagine you sitting. alone in happy sorrow.

your legs crossed. you wear a summer dress. blue. i refuse to be
the watcher. close my eyes. you shake the top leg. laugh eyes
full. submerge in loneliness. the writer leans on his arm. writes
in a small notebook. black ink. like those photos. you look off
into a distance of possibility. i rewind memory. in order to reload
a future. if you asked me. i would say yes. my lover struggles
over a line. covers and recovers. the natural light accompany-
ing shadow. you slowly unclothe her. your eyes close. you touch
the strap on her shoulder. brush it off her arm. your legs cross.
careless. i need to remember what it may have felt like. com-
plication. when he looks onto the world he witnesses old pho-
tographs. wheat grain. slowly push your dress down over your
breast. with my eyes closed. i see my lover. he is drawing. bent
over the paper as if my skin. his beautiful face. calm. lips parted
in kindness. remarkable. to believe he has drawn all over your
body. impossibilities. put your hand up to block the sun. at any
moment it might have happened. like looking into a mirror. i lick
your lips. salt dry. my lover smiles. anonymously. you remove
the dress. stand. stretch. your forearm rests atop your head.
casually. another color. blue shrouds. innocence. i look upon
my lovers body. breathe out a silent guilt. you lean back in the
chair. stretch your legs. cross ankles. if i had a camera. he thinks.
i could capture this moment forever. my lover brushes the side
of his face. i lie back in the sun. prevent alliances. concentration
arrives easily. as voices break against the ceiling and walls. frag-
mentation. of possible meaning. i close my eyes. so as not to
hear your body. never forgetting. a place. to replace. unlock the

coded bead work. she lounges knowing this desire drives. she needs no ones help. he hides. a shame. leaves rustle. a breeze shares whatever it is. click the shutter speed. lie.

my lover paints the world larger than life.

exaggerated. he wants to paint our bodies. black and white. de-
sires. he wants to bend me over the small step ladder. paint his
body inside mine. the long night. long. to taste trust. to swallow
fear. on the coffee table. he spills red wine on my chest. again. or
maybe hot coffee. i lurch up toward him. my lover paints desire
in bright colors. exaggerates. enters. releases. enters again. the
canvas. you wear the pink wig. blue summer dress. yellow high
heel sandals. the artist paints you into a woman. into a kind of
belonging to him. i lie waiting. unmoved. a pose. to tempt. in-
vite. his desire. my lover evaporates onto canvas. where i wait.
expectant. his beard. my neck raw burns. my lover holds me
down. his arm pushes against my back. his arm pulls my hip. my
lover an artist. he captures instances. in enlarged time. today.
tonight. your knees bruise. your mouth yawns. still. anticipate.
the artist pretends to have control. paints what he wants. leaves
brush strokes all over your posed body. i conjure him into my
bed at night. mimic painting. lie still. permit. his pleasure enters
your world. words cover the skin of my lover. he lies on his back.
uncovered. arms outstretched. words lick. tickle. he waits. pre-
tends. the artist holds your head. tight. between his bent legs.
acquiesce. give in to this comfort. she sits miles away. considers
a question. an answer. yes. he squeezes you tightly between his
hands and mouth. for a moment or two. a possibility. such bliss.
irrevocable change.

she sits alone. dreams a long way away.

in another state. in a place where snow falls deeply in april. blue. eyes. she pretends not to notice when you think about her. your thoughts remain black and white. you curl her toes under the blanket. the artist smokes. looks out on the snow covered mountains. solitude talks all of the time. she wants to ask you a question. it cannot be answered. the writer fills a page. feels preposterous. attacks his coffee. sorts through a kind of meaning. this month has been good for that. after an interlude. she shakes her head. no. she will leave it unasked. it becomes too much. your fiction. your story. water bathes her head. warm crystalline. he rushes to the table. rubs his eyes sore. hazel. recalls a mark on your neck. the artist fumbles through brushes. spills dark water. wants to land in another country. my lover fondles me in his thoughts. cooks dinner. pink heels go with so little today. except black. it is amazing. the promise. when flowers bloom.

i ask my lover to return me to my body.

she runs in the snow. exhilarate. my lover cannot remember. he has lost his way. moves quietly out of the room. i transfix story to what might possibly be read. as real. she lunges after a comparable love. asks me. savor. you approach. take her in eye sight. blue. hazel. still the current desire. affair. displace meaning among coffee cups. saucers. my lover cries softly in the loamy night. fear a product of this love. our lives. she withstands you. lets her clothes collect around the bed. at night you rub solitude onto your soft skin. piano mountains. betrayal. this cannot end well. his desire. the man with long fingers. grace. the artist puzzles over direction. like a destiny. listens closely. i succumb to fatality. move my lips as if miming something forgotten. my lover stumbles onto an idea. ties my thoughts to the chair with blue rope. i can no longer withstand struggle. she transforms into reflection. you.

when i am with you i feel finally at home.

safe. at peace. a little more to ask for. one cigarette. reprieve. you hold me close. tears. he wants this so badly. strangers elope around me. dance fanciful. in fear. you block their eyes. he feels fragile. afraid. too alone. always. she pushes her long hair back. her shoulders illuminated. the sun. you hold me close. whisper a word. a name. solitary. i hear across the great plains. across the rocky mountains. in the wind. your voice. he turns to see. but only spring snow. only wind. clouds. a man crumples to the ground. agony. solitude. longing. she runs through the desert streets. smiles by strangers. her intellect frees her. enables her to erase her body. those stares. you walk toward me. motion me to stand. touch my arm. my face. love. protect. she wears a beige blouse. her shoulders. illuminate. he smiles when he sees you. pretend everything will be all right. the same night you come to my bed. when you say. everyone i love ends up leaving me. i can not understand. despair. failure. we rock all night longing. the strangers. their voices rush through the room. point accusing fingers. point. whisper. sweat drenches her clothing. she bends over breathless. your lungs ache. how to spell a word out of existence. how to pretend a belonging. i pose my body. see in the mirror her eyes. blue. reflecting back. my body suddenly beautiful. with you he always feels beautiful. in place. my lover laughs. deep. sonorous. he paints naked. wears work boots. alone. against cold floor. a piano improvises. escapes stasis. fluencies. she disappears under a bright blue and yellow awning. the sun scorches. absorbs. you manipulate my words into a body. paint becomes for hours like this. outside the heavy spring snow. trees break. and she wears butterfly wings. hums along the piano. some made up melody. a young girl is afraid to play with other children. doubt pays an upbeat moment. uncanny. fleeting as any other memory. you recede. disappear. belong to me no longer. she turns a page. reenters the books world. of probabilities. outcomes. to change the world. promise. words fill the night air like stars.

he sits at a table. near the back.

awaits her arrival. he believes this may be what it feels like. the kind of slow dying. he withstands. arrives into temptation. i can only watch. i can only imagine. she begins to talk. toward him. my lovers sleek body radiates a new canvas. i lower myself down onto him. no brevity. no time. no longer awareness. flowers bloom. a photograph. black and white. she walks outside the frame. face hidden. obscured. inappropriate. i know what pain such love feels. my lover hugs me to the ground. i know the sound of such fear. so many others. wander in circles. a breeze. trees. nothing ordinary or expected. her smile a piano melody in blue. his eyes brown. open wide. hope. in line with lungs and blood. the artist repeats a common form. shape a mouth into words. uncompromised. she returns his glance. slides onto the adjacent chair. smiles. mystification begins. impermanence. legacy of sorrowful ribbons. grace. piano notes take butterfly wings. soar. fact.

i take photographs of an empty body.

a self to portrait. skin smooth. white. hair tangled. i pose a body in the feminine. shutter through an hour. to get what may be seen before. approach. left arm rests on head. right covers nipple. the hand. some force to compel an out. loud. enlivening a moment or two. aside the past. a story in hiding. enable a mask to take cover. a contorted truth. he looks into the camera. coyly. left shoulder shrug. like he has seen her do. i take photos of an empty body. sans identity. purpose. an other constructed still. when my lover elopes into my skin at night. i feel a sense of fleeting permanence. every time. the whispered threat. the i love you aloud among flashes of stars. you listen. piano background. a lovely womans voice. always a same as truth. his face cracks. eyesight dims. no one knocks. no one to answer. the question door out of this reality. out of reach. she calms a storm cloud. ruffles clothing. takes out an eraser. i pause. pick up paper. revealed. my lover enjoys opening me to horizontal light. rain. city. he takes his time. puts me back together. a new canvas. just begun. to get it right this time. he says. you smile as a stranger walks by. familiar face. mistaken. a look-alike. alternative. she can no longer tell. where this ends. where that one begins. feel secure in the lie. subordinate. remain outside power. outside his affection. pink denotes.

often i read a book for one sentence.

one word. a momentary solution. betrayal. you laugh and dance
with a stranger. she marks each footfall with exhilaration. a
small note eased into melody. butterfly wings. desire. were you
here we might cook dinner. smile. piano keys. memory faults de-
sign. perfects a pink moment. orange. you grab onto an outline.
a boundary between yet again. spoken under the breath. viola
touch to skin alive. she walks through a city. friendly already.
and it must be all right. to be. listen. traffic. a green. a yellow.
a long red. weep children. collage. image. discharge. when my
lover looks. my body crawls into deep wonder. night. might it
not already be over. concluded. rather open the wooden door.
enter back into strong arms. glisten tongue. speak words. out of
weight with. clothes. paintings. drawers open slight alive. wait
for him. wait on the longing body. wait.

you swell for his strong. perfect skin.

perfect day. all night i carry my lovers swollen desire. while outside the stranger looks in. watches. an open window. reflection. mirror. and my lover extreme. to want surrender. such want. i surrender. he watches. eyes aglow. brown. fugitive. furtively dreams his way into my bed. again fear. again. i glance around. wonder who this man is. the stranger. who i become in his created world. my lover complacent. stares bodily at a new canvas. wants more. more. the stranger thrusts toward me. deranged. afraid. what this all may mean. to him. my lover hovers over my tight body. skin smooth. like in the black and white photograph. waiting. exploding star fire. go get it. come get me. she speaks softly in sleep.

abandon means to enjoy piano.

means to sew weeping fabric into squares. into circles. here's the deal. find a first class postage stamp you have to lick. she dreams of traveling in a world that surprises women. safe. my lover scrubs the floors and walls. testament to. descend. tremble. stumble onto a hidden moment. enter aware. open blue. open brown. she shakes in the excitement of young childhood. you remember when the world was still new. how the tongue felt against his skin. a first time. i sit alert to the nothing that may become danger. arrange flowers. groom. check the time to go. driven always onward. today his earlobes ache. means someone speaks dully about him. a night ago you brush your smooth legs against hers. a room full of secrets opens. sigh again his name under your breath. the writer surrenders certain words in hopes to seduce. he stumps around for hours until the time suddenly moves into before. my lover and i stand together. our faces invisible. hazel. he takes my belt. unbuckles. lowers my pants to the floor. entangles my legs. every time. that's all it ever takes. and butterfly wings. a glass. tomorrow he throws you onto the step ladder. meaning a binding friendship. superstition. formidable. my lover moves into my body. my pores cry yes. yes. yes. he always knows. he must reside in your mind. in your memory imagined. as known. she kisses a foreign tongue and tumbles into a certain future. a story. she laughs and a room explodes in light. presume unless told otherwise. he's beautiful with his studied hat and leather jacket. my lovers eyes are brown. throbs. see how they love each other. parsley. my lover captures my arms tight above my head. pleasure interrupts. the writer is on fire.

bright golden shards of hopelessness. intercedes. she warms the cup. rinses. begs to come in. you check the door locks. the mad man dances in circles around the street light. rages appropriate. i fall asleep in his arms. dream a color canvas. black and white mirror image. she sips tea. wonders how to respond.

i sit across the table from you. alone.

i sit in light blue. memory plays what has not occurred. she looks on fondly. laps improbably language. a lovers dialogue. in other words. what is not presented. cannot be. so far beyond. my lover smiles. my body folds. we fondle desire. entertain this testament. he laughs aloud. brings stars to their knees. i fold my body onto. the step ladder. you lotion my body rub. holy. holy. holy. you begin entering. this our conversation. of signs. of mirror moans. you sit across the table. she smiles. tells you about fragmentation. outside the madman wears caution stickers. covers his suit. carries a sign. hate them. beware. my lover uses his impeccable teeth. she moans floating farther away. the writer picks up your book. looks for one particular sentence. one word. to ground. to be a reality. tremolo. she plays melancholic allusion. a summer meadow. i open myself. belong to my lover. completely. perfect. she plays a solitary note. that fills the bodies of these two men. encompasses. rapture. brown blaze with hazel. manufacture. some story. sky blue. an angel labors under the weight of space. my lover carries me over the bright night ceiling. butterfly wings dust horizontal.

an older man enters the bedroom.

the younger man strains over an old book of poetry. the older man touches his shoulders. invites an invasion of alternative endings. the writer begins. scribbles on a used page. new words. invented inventory. glory. a new moon half-sky life. use liminal. twilight. use interstice. dissolve the two more closely. their peppered speech. encoding centuries alone. to protect. to project bodies entwined. asleep now. resonant lovers. two men. on this precise day. elope convention. to simply be for now. and just as suddenly a child strikes her head and is gone.

he looks at photographs of his lover tonight.

whose perfect body caught in perfect sorrow. a last night. our last night. and i listen to the music. a piano outside lasting. pass across his chest. notice the two or three day beard. his earlobes. lovely shirted arms. entire region of longing. i must leave. don't you see. in order to save them both. such lonely looking. such hollow smile. he wraps himself in the memory. like snow images. a still city night. november say. and he wakes you. to take a shower with him. but it cannot work. desperation already narrating. i study the black and white photos. to hear the briefest word. a fragmentary hope. against. on the phone she speaks softly. assures you. there can be a place for all of this. i look back at my lovers strong body caught in dance. arms outstretch. belonging for those hours. later you permit him entrance. to wake you. roll you onto your side. work his way back into your delicate body. and both our hearts cry out. and the morning light already chasing them away. pushing him out of your house. back into solitude. into that prelingual world where temperance pretends. she loves you. you understand. how light bends around your lovers body. explodes in colors on the floor.

no need to hurry. they have all night.

they have this time. for the rest of their lives. their lives. he manages to slow anxiety. that want that drives him every night. to your attic room. but tonight. not tonight. he undresses quietly. watches your soft breath. the various hesitations. such calm reserve. he sits on your bed. watches. afraid to wake you. understands night language allure. he will rest as you fill his mind with peace. how it should always be. i dream of my lover sitting next to me. as i sleep. his eyes fixed on my breathing. brown. how my body rises and relaxes. finally he touches. tentative. warm skin smooth. the neck. lobe. you rustle quietly. roll closer. sleep deep soft sonorous. my lover touches my neck. lobe. i feel spring butterfly wings. hazel. tangerine. encompass. he slips next to your body. your back against him. he slowly unwraps you. into their pleasure. this pleasure. you feel him slip inside. moment by moment. you arch toward him. wrap your right leg around his. want pulls them both into this a becoming. there is no hurry. cannot be. this night embrace. he pushes. slows. pulls. while you circle delight around him. take all of him. words fall apart. this world encourages. they move as if in primitive memory. a piano. one soft note at a time. resonant minor. my lover moves me toward him. moves into me. envelops my body with his breathing. to dance. to want to dance. this dance. the night so young.

there are people who slide so silently through their lives.

they are easily missed. you are like that. invisible. yet. in the black and white photograph. present. he sees you from the side. knees curled into your chest. camera eyes. his tenderness pushes anger out the door. a passing car. moments collect as webs in corners of the room. often i ignore even the loudest warning. prefer perfect silence. he dislikes every aspect of his life. a young woman sits to your right. legs crossed on the chair. he cannot take his eyes off the sliver of skin. between sweater and skirt. how can any of this not be possible. i bore easily. unhappy. with life. change so quiet it feels distant. a door squeaks. open. another mans voice. i feel my lovers absence. my dreams dark stone. cold. she buys clothing. sans wire. runs wildly even though her legs break. into orange pain. my lover believes my death will still the acrylics. i marvel at a hint of spring rain.

i wonder where you have gone.

the piano silent. he looks back at time. searches some insight. a light. when my lover drives across kansas. late night. a solitary farmhouse. could you have believed. a simple loss marks meaning. she pirouettes. takes him into her arms. to forget. could you have but known. to simply and again. lick your body into her name. correctly whisper. a black dog sniffs around a tree. rings run around the block. an end to some sensibility. do you hear. a lone figure. blue. i hear your voice in french. what you are saying. it may have been real. and you dream at night. his age like brittle glass. enraptures her into meaning something. delightful. this time of year. earlier a small spider. i love you. circumstance of externals. newspapers. a bag. pink. sweat earth grays. too long ago. in black and white. forestall color. keep at bay. he doesn't even mind failure. but forgetting. the crime of complacency. she wraps a shawl of change around her shoulders. a poet brings us into her world. violence. and children. death near. brown. lavender. a way of seeing. when outside the house. still remains kind. i can no longer do this. you think while tapping your right foot.

there can be a suffering like candy.

she stands outside talking to friends. her ankles ache from too much unusual convention. not you. want. to join the fun. sit alone still. they cannot see you. can only imagine safety. where there are no men. his lover pretends to be dreaming. he takes your arms and legs. binds them. soft clarity. i watch from a distance. listen to foreign words. my neighbor bores easily. lights a cigarette. he cannot understand. that i sometimes look beautiful. in a blue dress. pink. i revel in illusionary. my lover comports my body into salvation. on the mouth. amazing red.

he must know i move farther away than night breeze.

the body marks a lost path. she looms in the next room. sweater drapes her left shoulder. allure. in a look. closely. enough time lapse. save scratches the door ajar. charge lightning air cadence. next. i cannot move. to continue as it has been. always. the impossibility. for what is a love. sans passion. stay waiting. to be wanted. to be taken. desired. like death. to still dreams. incorporate a joined grief. disagreeable. like a kind of longing. she wraps her broken heart in blue laughter. leaves me broken. a lie. but the words. sometimes they bleed. she reads. and her blood flows. you sit in wonder. might such a joy voice power. the hallway tips slightly downward. fear grasps. ineptitude. adore. red sports bra. arms outstretch. jesus. in that place. to wait. perch. she will visit. again. dark brown. hazel blue. alone.

emptiness. the words. surround.

cover floors. scrawl. a door opens. shuts. wind power. you approach gray. with color thought. say blue. say brown. she lies. waits his improbable return. act or lose. she says. sleep incorporates a sound. like piano. can any thought occur. beyond previous one. miss a piece. a puzzle dulls. my lover stretches canvas. lifts my arms. with rope taut. spreads legs. easel desire. tonight i hold you in my hands. precious. a spell. or in other words. to be always alone. a stranger. leave a message. wrong number. wail. while rain simply falls. in line. her eyes embrace. sorrow palpable. brilliant. another visual move. wipe your body down. ice water. wake up to a tomorrow. it may be that. sorrowful voices repeat. over and over. i suppose i like her legs the best. nice neon caper. lost current. whisper truth under their breaths. if they would only apply themselves. multiply. of endings. of purity. a red car perhaps. old torn photographs. memories and forgetting. strawberries. afghanistan order. may i disrobe your fear. my lover enters from behind. and i wake outside. though inside. a gift certificate love. can it be real. sans bodies. ours. with purpose. draw a scheme on newsprint. wire a few dollars. donate. still remember. on one of the first nights. when you touch him. and know immediately. pretend a survival. today we touch hands. an intimate moment gathers rainbows. butterfly wings. dye hair. pink zeros. hard around an edge. a space. draw cancer on her naked body. stars. my lover thinks. you look beautiful in blue. orange. smile while the chance permits. so far down. like i said. become less brief. roll around chocolate.

it is and as in death.

words crawl around the floor. ants. lemon juice. she saddens each day. knows it's over. not even butterfly wings. not even blue. brown. he elongates truth to fit a point. misremembers experience. we are all suddenly caught. in headlight glow. pre-occupation. ourselves. primary. and why not laugh. loud as you want. he draws a life he has never known. events evaporate into fiction. like your love affair. my lover loses sight. meets a crowd delusion. find it difficult to discover. a hard truth. my departure. she wraps an idea around your body. like forever. an image in monotones. i cannot find even one unused word. the actress dies. mono chrome gender desire. near as self-evident. you fall onto the ground. uncontrollable grief. like any other disappoint-ment. who would want to stop you. affixed as he is in imaginary world. and of grandeur. goodbye. lost in the vacuous black hole of his pupils.

he sees. to be. that is like. a kind of normal.

to be the boy. his father expected. she dances on tiptoes. flies above terror. he looks on. like blue. suddenly an ocean. or not the sky. you flirt with a difficult decision. to let him go. on. or toward a remaining complacency. my lover looks in the mirror. sees only nothing. like a past history. and becomes solitude. whenever time growls. elongates. the ground cowers. butterfly wings. she smiles. plays an old country song. piano brown. check the lessoning slack key. you observe. recollect some other location. locution. to make her figure. darling. a time to relax. a kind of like a waiting. the more looking forward. burn more photos. water damage. erase a time. before. his story again. the artists only concern. to manipulate acrylic desire. drop glass. shards the size of heartbreak. blood burn awakens. you marvel. a few marble steps. a relief. a sigh size. seize. she walks back and forth. wears black and white. like photography. like a blank page. orange. a kind of backward glance. the writers dumb stone stare. recalcitrant. relapse. mirror nod. she lovelies a part today.

try to bring things about. to hide once more.

fortification denial. a stranger holds you at bay. presume she needs protection. group perception. the shoes i bought when with you. conditional. full languish. fleshy. remarkable story enlarging the room. still music accompanies. a slow piano. eventual ornamental desire. i wrap my naked. await visitation arms. visions of cloud bodies. delicate red wine. to belong. again. finally. she smiles a new world. forget the momentary. lull. cross back against traffic. listen even more attentive. confinement. pretend a more happens. soft spring snow. brittle ice love. life. never a mere only. never a grouped together. never really here runs its course. already near a losing. hold tightly. cup your hands upon his heart. pain an outside window. see brown. blue. see black and white. see semblance of breast. watch the star fall pain. encumbered. i'm usually pretty out of it. he thinks in fragments. like simple sentences. a bloody mole. bright smooth skin. soft memory. hold time up to the light. longitudinal. blinds fabricate moments. escape into monotonous. horizons. you lie on the floor. whose shadow dies. hazel memory. long toward an outwards. while words spill all over the table. drip margins onto the floor. the writer misses it all. seeks in another direction. watches. the point. my lover ties me onto a stretched canvas. an easel secret. he says to me. a sparkled now. a physical movement. he dies trying to run over a train. whispers recede. a small child smiles. she knows a secret too. understands. his eyesight wayward glance. a beautification. like your name forgotten. one exciting instance. to be. my lovers incessant. room full of predictable sorrow.

you wonder as speech proceeds.

can your father hear your words. the things you say about him. ghostly. a flicker in darkness. brightens. then dulls to black and white photographs. he might have been incapable of love. that passion filled with want. she remains nearby. a party of more. ignore the age difference. difficult. another form of lack. cling rather to procedures. to desire. mean absence. to want. what remains lacking. she cleans a table. stacks boxes. you look out the window. a promise of more spring snow. allusion. my lover finds in the everyday. routine. comfort. reads words meant to transpire. his beautiful dark heart opens. invites body. talk to me today. say what needs saying. an upright piano. you give her a beautiful ring. he finds a necklace studded in bright greens. blues. a diamond or two. like cut glass. commerce enjoys consent. in the tattoo you find fleeting memories. she enjoys your sex. just not enough. a sign of their time. overlook. i wear a dirty shirt. to visit becomes intoxicating. an old man falters. falls to the ground. a young childs fantasy elopes. try to pick the red thread up. hiding in the carpets woven secret. not to be out done. my lover presses his hips. against an unwilling accomplice. acrylic props undo temerity. invites entrance. low piano notes. yes. she scrambles up the side of a mountain. imagines inventing a solid power. resolute. dives populate the still evening air. you are missing. he feels the emptiness of afterwards. an unexpected guest cooks laughter. prepares dessert. sleep tickles your left arm. light folds over the night breeze. the writer sits. a ghost. page erasure. declare ones living. you cannot. to mouth his name. might suddenly. make appearance possible. can no one ever finally know. you wonder. speak the song aloud. might becomes a suffering moment. a movement under. gloss covers their lives. lies to wait patiently. my lover reaches through the figured canvas. searches for his lovers impossible gift. be willingly present. approach an end. another canvas to stretch. belong to. a word scrambles toward breath. you laugh too loudly. some say. as if longing the only reasonable season. beards grow like wild trees around her. listen. carefully. she hears a distant sound. as if voices rising pink. like an orange aglow. old monochrome photos. irrelevance. misremember. an important event. she enters. walks toward him. while you. heart flames their disguise.

he stores his soul in boxes.

kept in storage unit. she travels lightly. reflects anticipation. there being always another place to locate. match the plane to air. he listens for signs of better. leaps toward the screen door. flies. spider web intersect. meaning. corpses. my lovers long fingers speak acrylic. canvas. commingle with longing. disappearing memory. unpacking one box. he discovers. she lingers in mountains. make the best of situation. circumstance. dwell nicely inside a crook. make believe fantasy more real. fiction. graphic absence. where words skip a heartbeat. where my lover touches surfaces. where she only fills one partial void. hold your breath. under water stream. piano drum machine. drive farther ahead. anticlimax. shoulder bare in early spring. sudden sun light. threaten more snow figures. above a door take on semblance. brown. temporary blue. more likely yellow. hazel alarms confusion. ask commonly. how have you been. she may be lovely. boxed as she is in subordinate illegality. perfect word of a you submerged. simple how a kiss refracts. frayed edges embark. accoutrement learning. it's either a leaning toward. or away. to hold too firmly. what begins as simple correspondence. evanescent lies. in a corner. beyond well lit lines. successive remarks gain a foothold. the writer lounges in unfolding prose. enfolds unremarkable gains. a stretched current. orange. a kind of pink. only not so. ice. coffee. eviscerate. hold back revelation. guarantee unhappiness. north so much more than. to penetrate. to be found thus. my lover walks calm breaths. inspire. premature ejaculate.

your every day turns into conditional.

everyone else wants to help. but never like it begins. remember to tell him. it's over. that an absence unattended abscesses. relationship not only to the mouth. wake up. turn the morning on platform heels. when you get a chance. check it out. fuchsia. earlier she loads the car. heads out in still morning darkness. if only light might lead onward. so easily. my lover coughs. a fit of rage. fades into blue. brown. she smiles. butterfly wings. he sits at a table. writes it all down. what kind of life is that. on tuesday you embellish your right arm. figurative ink stains. he is so beautiful. you often wish you were home. is that what you did. okay. interesting process. the man talks academically. which is to say. positions himself superior. authority. as more than mere. rewind the narrative function. pretend it has never happened. yet. pretend the world fresh. a first morning. that he is not preemptive. to hear himself talk. i would fold my body into yours. be accompaniment. companion. correspondence on the cusp of your lips. never say i already know. at times she worries. writes aloud. i cry too much. my lover walks to his studio. barely clothed. arrangements. willow blue. she wraps her eyes onto the page. believes in words power. to in sight. insist. simply put. to continue as if it really does mean. more. in relation to. try to cast a lisp onto an idea. come back to the page. some articulated old lover. embellished. wisdom comes in many forms. he links illusion to fiction. masks her mouth shut. a piano shoots panes of warm gloss. cover your eccentricity. entire. my lover says i love you beneath his closed eyelids. saffron slips. onto the table top from above. i think. this time it's real. believe it. life without art. is like living dispassionate. which is not emotion. which is always drama. he used to believe. if enough people believed in love. it would come about. wrong from the start. nobody seems to like those shoes. all the more reason to wear them.

those lips. begin with that.

and a scent of britney spears. overload the boat. buoyancy chal-
lenge. pretend they don't look like the jokers. that other dead-
beat. madman. remember ink dries. even under skin. cast your
safety net. hold hands. and prayer. won't make a difference.
but in the effort might. she has nice legs. what does it matter.
you stop by. you don't. i wait. i don't. in the end it remains.
alert to sound of emptiness. a few years. days. never precise-
ly. the same. my lover entertains fictions. of our place. remains.
together. piano. butterfly wings. she wears beauty. as if born
into it. hold hands. pray. for what good. to come or not. never
license to own. this time cobalt. or bright like green. door hinge.
squeak a memento. to pause. whisper. my god. may. some one
once. over weight. enamor gravitas. his good right eye. bright
blizzard diamonds. crack her yoke. willing. she returns to what
feels familiar. like a wedding dress. when you kiss me. feel my
whole body. entire. enter you. say. yes god. again. please. she
tattoos graffiti onto his skin. memoriam. clear your throat. write
as if to pursue. turn him down. the man wears sleeveless. a kind
of dress shirt. she climbs ever higher. exhilarate. so long as you
don't leave the ring. behind. made to jump head first. paradise.
deliberation synesthesia. again cobalt. like a kind of dark white.
remove your shoes. count a way to toes. sparse pull. the sky un-
wraps. stars more or less random. my lover. i am your plaything.
she wraps desire. tight. like an ill fitting dress. scamper to his
arms awaiting. believe. what other of course illuminated. words
time out. express no concern. already as if it never happens. she
risks. folds her body. over mirror glass. sends reminders out be-

fore her. he says he has a photo. he knows you'll love. find already five in black and white. titillation. always only a frequent respite. on any newsstand. try to end it wild. wild oscillation. can they possibly emanate. she wings forward. inside a large powerful beast. able to beat the bet. against their kind. morality. he waits to cut his hair. until she leaves.

she speaks with a childs voice. maturity delusion.

both breasts missing. mass. he wanders through the room. call it monday. gray. sub-tone of spring. rain. misery. wake him up with your hand. decide. instantly. upon a show of warm need. flick the smoke. into the street. feel the patient wheel. to return. could either have known. how long. long legs. white mini. common pursues even into wilds. charm a smile. break out. the skin. a memory. like muscle. she becomes more. in her absence. real. the writer worries over any word. remembers articles. every one counts. she said it would be nice. to cook a meal together. he waits. aside the dark cut. there may have been. a time. now many revoke. opening doors. today. saturated in words. clamoring for attention. nouns. to cover form. step outside of yourself. tomorrow gray hues. still life.

and after we fuck. the words. dull.

engage in hide-and-seek. pretend to having eloped. the window slightly ajar. smoke pushes. the screen rattles. it may be. on air. night breeze. ocean cool. he suspects you. thinks surely you have spoken to the woman. who dances in fear. on mountaintops. their relationship so changed. you push dark air. your lips part. european cigarettes. he reads her long green summer dress. this morning my lover wrote. i'll accept any form of being-near-you. my eyes fall. toward the ceiling. cold shuttered thought. it might yet be possible. you believe. five years from now. will you remember this. doubt supersede memory. even these. the words scramble toward a meaning. can't take that on. she promises. but never ends up. in your bed. he rereads the card. sent from another country. dancing figures. perhaps. it is not that difficult. growing old. quite natural. i have her paint. my toenails pink. opportunities. vicariously. you sense their excitement. it is about to begin. their dream together. look at the map. where to locate our budding. when my lover enters. my room. aflame in brilliant color. acrylic blue. brown. hazel. wings desire. summer tease. outside noon sunlight. fear competes. the hearts ache. i know you must feel. one of the lucky ones. time plays among children. pianos line the garage. see shapes. forget nouns. roll along. she waves. a smile breaks. careful melodic accompaniment. my lover only wants. to live with me. anywhere. as i have. necessitated. large portions of forgetting. to pretend. safety. to pretend. a belonging. the phone sits askance. atop the piano. return home. top off the wine glass. worry about tomorrow. or tuesday. as if any of it's. a done deal.

i think about you today. wonder what mountain you climb.

how sweat glistens. even more at that altitude. attitude. she worries that no lasts forever. while the yes pretends. only. longevity. you slip your sweater on. to stay warm. even late in may. with sunshine. some prefer stuffed chairs. pin your hair up. conspicuously male. to notice. he sits alone. writes back out of his world. when you reread his letter. your body falls into his hands. to be anywhere near you. rest in conversation. speak softly. flirt. my lover writes his longing. onto stretched canvas. forgotten sketches. where has it all gone. that living together loving. a stranger. walks by. the looks. your estranged friends. wife. hold the gray day. near their hearts. teeter on the brink. to bring this to life. try harder. that's what i thought. he was never particularly good. at small talk. i prepare to return. finally get to it. are you happy. yes. that's all that matters. your mother opens a purse. out spills heart fragments. and butterfly wings. tempt the other side of never. outside. he stands smoking. near a fire hydrant. trash can. the alley soaks up souls. gray. like a kind of orange. revenge. cold. insincere. greeting. a kind of apology. all the while you pretend. it's a kind of belonging effort. at times you forget. about the over. abandoned. to discover again. the childs exuberance. she climbs. stiff. rope dangles. recalls one particular. blue. moment. the ring a sign. yes. maybe. sometime wool. blue. green shoes. laughter. a hint of a possible joke. my lover moves slowly. willows paint. acrylic figures. a foreign tongue. he possibly understands. the lovers hold hands. ignore the bright red stares. impossible forgiveness.

outside the rain. cold. the older woman.

eyes creased in sorrow. her dead child. whisper almond thoughts. speak spiral blue. semblance. the pastry crumbles. her long legs. crossed at ankles. posed for photographer. quiet distills into a liquid. chill. air. tattoos. piano children. for grief shudders. always. my lover repeats. anywhere. so long as you. are nearby. not arizona. not arkansas. alabama. never montana. ugly states of mind. signifying. harm. there are those. whose mere presence. destroys a good mood. outside rain. chill air. a cigarette rests on the tables corner. little wind.

there is nothing. common. we all share.

perhaps mystery. nor even death. singular. individual. every
time. last year. he felt he'd never see you. again. that may. of too
many words. desperation. fear. he wanders. searches a voice.
one. in bright sunlight. have you already. gone there. this morn-
ing. my lover writes in flesh and agony. wants to know. where he
might lay his head. impractical joke. i want. more certain even.
than certain death. anyones. she bends her lens. down upon my
loneliness. a detail. among. the i love you. swirling above their
heads. a new tattoo. flakes. heals. my lover bends down. onto
me. sore soul rooted thus. you always knew. he'd end up living
alone. what to make of all this. rigor. or perhaps. not even stub-
born will. can bring her back. amidst turned pages. fragmented
language. look askance. four poorly clothed. women. figures
only. suggesting dance. imagined bliss. a flake of tattoo. taped
to the page. still. slow. saturday. deep inside. sits opposite the
heart. a growing gnawing sense. a. thing like emptiness. or love.
the photo. black and white. now rests on his right forearm. he
dreams. a stranger. a madman. attacks the two men. who walk
holding hands. the one pulls out a pen. kept in his pocket. stabs
him twice. writing a new. falling. blood poem. it is time. to write
a new narrative. moon. fiction. crowds sound out. silence.

it is not. as though love. matters.

is ever enough. the inner ache. worst. than. she remarks. i frequently desire. other strangers. having. meaning no one in particular. my lover states. you're my doctor. not ph.d. my family ignores this. my lover covers his hands. acrylic colors. wipes down then up. my body. hanging only because she thinks. i love her. does she move. inside with him. piano. jazz. the womans voice. echoes. reach back. into. through time. their memories. misaligned. drink more water. there's a solitary goldfish. whisper doubt. she walks along an air current. some pleasing. pleasure. to say stiff. to say upper lip. his tattoo peels. willing. the writer believes. it is enough. to simply report experience. as if trusted. stuff the top words. shallow. she leaves. outside memory. alternate melody. like hand made. like butterfly earrings. he did a pretty good job. on me. hand. a kind of blue. wash. detach retina. black and white. shades. his hair cut. shaved by friends. joke. her voice. the phone call. relax. refrain. bitterness questions the sky. yes. like yellow. like brown. or green. to buy. flower. small glass vase. they all. the others. try too hard. always. fail. among many. the younger.

after all these years. it is impossible.

to distinguish between. how people know. or believe they know. you. and your own sense. of self. few shades remain. grays. off white. she seeks. but he is already. gone. and the miles add up. out here. like some lost. continent. lost. my lover desires. forgiveness. i taste the eucharist. his body. wafer. replenish. change focal point. eliminate delusion. of depth.

it has happens before. his going to visit.

but never does. the litany of excuse. the clamor of denial. my lover desires. as a kind of dread. meaning runs rampant. fleets. blue occasions hope. you tire of being. paired to him. as not my lover. an act. a kind of rebellion. like chaos. she sits alone. writes unremarkable. her lived lives. as if real. again. or important. a kind of memory. meaning. the young woman sings. imagines a chainsaw. her arms. to destroy. she thinks. the armament of men. it happens. opportunity misunderstood. like black and white. in photographs. enlarging fear. he motors across. southern states. enlivened. love acts strangely. like a kind. of watching. want. denial. nasal conversation. end silence. divide. my lover wraps an idea. around my body. my lover. whose lean masculinity. frightens. listen carefully. she drives through. two straight nights. a sounds like. alarm. to try to live. outside cliché. turn the radio. off. there's dirt on the page. prescient assumption. he resents being coupled. understands. invitations only follow. him. because of the other. man. whose impression. of popularity builds illusion. get words in. between and edge. gloss surface. too old now. a time. fill breath. feel impressive. liken it to only. his pretension.

it is a day of complications. disruptions.

interruptions. phone calls. lawn machines. dreams. she seeks you out. like a kind of lyric poem. mouth out anguish. loss. a voice sings of soul. courage. my shoes new. i find your strong hands. appealing. to inflict. upon the body. honest bruising. appointment desire. passed from my lover. to me. as if a kind of in love. a kind of breathless. a taking. that gives. in the mirror she notices. a nothing akin to absence. a space beyond. and i could say this about me. never quite enough. out loud though. he wears out. it becomes all about. perspective. depth of field. gray tones. also silent. she dances in glowing spirals. circle teases. he disrupts a narrative. in order to. both make eloping gestures. you push beyond no. in order to a kind of hearing. a right answer. an alternative. feelings splayed. charcoal despair. intervals. gyrate.

with her you wander. your minds actions. temerity.

palatable. his lips full. inviting. whenever it might have been. possible to return home. but now. my lover works late. into early morning hours. his long fingers acrylic stained. he touches me. i go wild. into swordfish worship. some other problem. unveils. work the clay. damp. porous. his body. mine. integrate. allegory presence. like communal memory. when i have time. he thinks. or likes to think. from redundant practice. a kind of not seeing. like blinders. horizontal. quiet desperation. some call it family. familiar. when. the common enough loss. of a way. through. i don't even know myself. he likes to think. to himself. bed alarm. my lover wraps. his imagination. mine. flower poses. discourse against. salutation. when lavender scent. aroma of found bodies. like objects. intermittent. lie back down. time remains. before you must leave. the other one thinks. only grays. shades of menace. meaning. her voice carries itself. beneath resonances of other voices. like watching a sunset. when by oneself. a little bit like. circumspect. a being like a more. a phone number. shoes. caustic. my lover gropes in the dark. long fingers search. desire behind the door. or locked in attic. i want to help him. want to move. closer. they long in outrageous silence. may it never having been. requires a semblance. unapologetic synthesis. may be monday. she finds her home in words. still. here. performative. tattoo scabs. taped to paper edge. it is quiet. sleepy. when she walks in. her sister gathers strength.

aroma. like a mixture. of voices.

some laughter. as movement of a more. like a broken faucet. or. to die. is to quit. quite suddenly. archival footage. in black and white. nor surprises. enjoyment. outside. whenever the wind. aggressive. like a thinking. about loss. or the phone interrupting. contract. an otherwise memorable. occasion. a kind of rose. blue. when he was a child. you never recognize time. only change. earmarks. my lover. the artist. throws acrylics around canvas. spiral like loss of control. anger brutalizes. she uses a chainsaw. writes ferociously. word chips. cover them all. in brown. in hazel or green. the runner sweats profusely. her slim body. a must admit. a don't want this. with you. again. rather. to move out. of predictable. like a sudden head rush. but more constant. dialogue. ice cream. out of the closet. a last night. reverberates. like a to last. her beauty a standard ploy. learned. leave it all unsaid. elegant. project back into the mirror. reflect meaning. locate her hips. walk away. enormous relief. casual. ring for important. unhappy. resident advisor.

to be. with you. as a not. in fantasy.

but present. to know outside. tour around. to ask. instead view photographs. to remain. outside. not here. when as in fantasy. nor present. but backwards. mirrored as. in repetition. redundant. like a kind of dying. a want to know. you. what comprises. not just reaction. not just as. formative construct. a being. like a to detach. remember. precisely. right this moment. as not when reading. but to write toward. or outside sexual. as a thing. not here. nor you. to be with you. as a right now. in a blue event. a to be dying. not to be. present in viewing. not in to see. as educated. collective construct. privileged. not like saxophone. nor piano. being unattached. only on when called. nor photographic. black and white. which means. to signify grays. nor brown. hold cigarette. bud ripe vase. breast. let him in on it. to know a kind. of completion. over.

an old woman. the child behind. loudly plays.

she knees. on. overlook. overlooks. writing a person. tries like an ocean. no need. to worry. autumn like breath. or leaves. she. shoulders whose glow. dots. he signs relief. indigo. or a kind. lavender like. incorporate. small idea instants. instinct. she remarks. butterfly. wings my lover. desire. rope dreams. tattoo flirtations. fetish. espresso slips. gray. sun bright. like small hope rings. piano strums. a person. across street. or as people gather. like silent. in prayer elopement. in to conventions. like common language. like sweaty pits. foreheads glistening. a chance. as if in change. a dollar. and parking ticket. to want. as a going outside. a to wait. clear instead. locked. fragrant line. upon dawn a spatial. tendency. a clean as frequency. piano. thrum. to word incredible. a liken to dying. breathe. insecurity. horizon. in green. in brown like hair. gray. she invents. arms. legs fills. nameless. unless use found. to be mere. less. ambulance. echo lights. a wait. busy traffic. occurrence. memorable. as a such. in like. royal. eyes scatter. to clarify. my lover. likes to dream. a. together. time walk oceanic. breathe breeze thunder. sock skin line. indentation. place. broken. in fridge. back score. victorious. as in. a need. more. placed as mere. reflection. a counting to five. to spell a brief. silhouette caramel. haircut. articulated. enormous. it is easiest. in to believe as. an image understanding. not near. as in a language. balloon. fragmentary. in moments. synchronize.

it is as if. coming. into. darling.

pastels. bloom petals. enlarge. encompass solitude. in pink like a. ink on skin art. tattoo drum machine. heavy legs. beautiful. and a young. like poetry. storm. flooding. wording worry. oil spill. shoulder bone. we all enter. into a their. like a thin. air. coming. say. the i'm sorry. cough backfire. reflex drill laughter. iron bars. windows. door. insurance. plates. fingers. balloons butterfly wings. to mean. a hard working neon green. sliver blue. with peanut butter scone. in a too long. my lover opens. ladybug. fly away. reminders as construct. like a second present. he lounges. a deck chair rhapsody. in bright acrylic thoughts. urgencies. blue. rapture gateway. entrance. hazel. brown. as if a kind of. making love. as meaning a more. only. than to. a mere. to be fucking. like gesture. or entrapment. meaning pleasurable. elongation. time stretch. shards in shredding. action. invisible. indigo. lavender. tulip tongues. melodic piano rest. with cheese. in a like reading. she. completes an into. forgotten or silence. like open red. a color page. like a black lab. tail. outside. or brush hair back. ice cubes. night semblance agreeable. agenda. location. as in outdoors. being more than. when he sees. you. they all swarm being. totality. detachment. irks knowledge. askance. in an hour. like relation of among. blue intelligence. brown beauty. than. brawny scrutinize. some more. timeless recall. exquisite cloud cover. in shadow. like flattery curtains. or blinders. she searches for a name. stays clean like glass. you smoke. rain fabricates. the look of black and white. film. service space spin. a second one. better. than photographers appeal. authority. to stop. smoking begin to. before.

noise. as children. shrill.

she wipes wood chip sweat. beams in blue. orgy. you envelop. stop to wave. recently my lover. leave with two boys. lag behind. to not. in simple describe. removal. to but be calls. any things. of interest. later drive. flitch past. in rig. or oil spill. she fails. careful no part. of being as. when in alive. wait to eat. silence sudden. rain storm. piano voice. accompaniment. walk onto leaves. scene. orange. like poppies. blooming water frame. parking ticket. sell that. exchange. he refers to her. as a he. knows better. you shrug. earlier. having them. call her faggot. all light laughter. around. room fills. anonymous. attackers. sudden safety joy. shakes. you hand her. a small stone. thrown around. somewhere else. his ears plug. mute sounds. not only like. a screaming diplomacy.

my lover slices triangles in my wrists.

because i don't flinch. acrylic colors pulse onto. atop a new perfect painting. the canvas ruined. he says. rolling me in a plastic drop cloth. love resembles a need. to lift pain toward the blue ocean. nor stars peppering dawn. she looks right through you. toward another man. strangers make anonymous howls. at one the writer flees. scratches at the new tattoo. scabs. place one wafer on your tongue. think about.

i consider running away. with a growl. with a thought possible.

like an image. two dimensional. like a tiny bicycle tire. or a disrupted chain. you wear your hat black. a kind of storefront bad guy. impossible not to. know what they say. call me or obscene. she struggles along. climbs like a running. not away. there remains a purple toward. accountability. violin bow tie. even at fifty. weight matters. as in fabricated care. darling. it wilts too easily today. upbeat pop song. lift permission. her back aches. heart broken bible story.

Grateful acknowledgment is given to the editors of the following journals for first publishing the following poems:

RiverSedge: "he sits holding his head between his eyes." and "he feels a meager sense of place since he left you."
The Rockford Review: "he doesn't mind the world now that he's removed his glasses."
Ginosko: "aroma. like a mixture. of voices.," "he is lost. i am lost. in amazement.," "you find it impossible to understand.," "she speaks with a childs voice. maturity delusion.," and "tonight i am writing into you."
Voices Israel: "i consider running away. with a growl. with a thought possible.," and "i wonder how you behaved when your sister died."
The Bicycle Review: "and after we fuck. the words. dull." and "as usual morning takes on an air of metonymy."
Wilderness House Literary Review: "one awaits. an arrival. a movement or two prior."
Cedilla V: "he sits at a table. near the back.," "i take photographs of an empty body.," "often i read a book for one sentence.," "you swell for his strong. perfect skin.," and "abandon means to enjoy piano."
Cedilla VI: "you feel exposed. in the open. revealed."
Cirque: "you wonder as speech proceeds."

A special thanks to Robert Paul Cesaretti and Maggie Heaps for including "aroma. like a mixture. of voices.," in *Ginosko Anthology #3.*

gary lundy was a professor of English and Creative Writing at The University of Montana Western, in Dillon, Montana. He retired in 2011. Each July he is one of the instructors of the mandolin building class at Rocky Grass Academy, in Lyons, Colorado. He is the author of: *this making i tore the sight from* (Sweetbrier, 1996); *lavish is say nothing like again* (Blue Malady, 1997); *to each other water cool and pure* (Blue Malidy, 2003). His fourth chapbook, *when voices detach themselves*, was published in the fall of 2013 by is a rose press. He lives in Missoula, Montana.